ROM. OF THE WESTERN CHAMBER

A Musical

by Howard Rubenstein & Max Lee

Book and Lyrics by Howard Rubenstein
based on S. I. Hsiung's translation
of the thirteenth-century Chinese play *Xi Xiang Ji*
attributed to Wang Shifu and/or Guan Hanqing

Music by Max Lee
based on traditional Chinese folk music
selected by Howard Rubenstein
and adapted and arranged by Max Lee
with original music by Max Lee
and Howard Rubenstein

Granite Hills Press™

ROMANCE OF THE WESTERN CHAMBER
A Musical

by Howard Rubenstein and Max Lee

Book and Lyrics by Howard Rubenstein based on S. I. Hsiung's translation of the thirteenth century Chinese play *Xi Xiang Ji* attributed to Wang Shifu and/or Guan Hanqing. Music by Max Lee based on traditional Chinese folk music selected by Howard Rubenstein and adapted and arranged by Max Lee with original music by Max Lee and Howard Rubenstein.

© Copyright 2008, 2012 Howard Rubenstein. *All rights reserved.* Unauthorized reproduction in any form including but not limited to written, performance, or recording is a violation of copyright except for short excerpts in reviews or references where the author and book title are credited or as permitted under the U.S. Copyright Act of 1976. Address inquiries to publisher Granite Hills Press™. Royalty fees are set upon application in accordance with producing circumstances.

Published by Granite Hills Press™ 2012.
First edition:
        ISBN 978-1-929468-28-7   (10 digit ISBN 1-929468-28-8)
        Library of Congress Control Number: 2011930269
[A preliminary edition was published by Granite Hills Press™ as a spiral bound script, 2011.]

   e-mail: granitehillspress@yahoo.com
   http://www.granitehillspress.com/
   SAN 298-072X

Cover by Chuck Conners

Printed in the United States of America

Components of

ROMANCE OF THE WESTERN CHAMBER
A Musical
by Howard Rubenstein and Max Lee

ROMANCE OF THE WESTERN CHAMBER A Musical:
BOOK
ISBN 978-1-929468-28-7 (ISBN 10: 929468-28-8)
ROMANCE OF THE WESTERN CHAMBER A Musical:
MUSICAL SCORE
ISBN 978-1-929468-19-5
ROMANCE OF THE WESTERN CHAMBER A Musical:
MUSICAL SCORE Volume 2
ISBN 978-1-929468-25-6
ROMANCE OF THE WESTERN CHAMBER A Musical:
PARTS
ISBN 978-1-929468-21-8
ROMANCE OF THE WESTERN CHAMBER A Musical:
REHEARSAL SCORE
ISBN 978-1-929468-20-1
ROMANCE OF THE WESTERN CHAMBER A Musical:
CD EXCERPTS
UPC 8-84501-30209-8, ISBN 978-1-929468-15-7
ROMANCE OF THE WESTERN CHAMBER A Musical:
CD THE TENOR'S SONGS
UPC 8-84501-48668-2, ISBN 978-1-929468-18-8
ROMANCE OF THE WESTERN CHAMBER A Musical:
CD
UPC 8-84501-44834-5, ISBN 978-1-929468-16-4
SONGS FROM RUBENSTEIN AND LEE'S ROMANCE OF
THE WESTERN CHAMBER A Musical:
CD
UPC 8-84501-78357-6, ISBN 978-1-929468-27-0
Printed and recorded in the United States of America

PLAYS

BY HOWARD RUBENSTEIN

AGAMEMNON: A Play by Asechylus, Translated from the Greek into English, with Introduction, Notes, and Synopsis, with Reconstructed Stage Directions. ISBN 978-1-929468-07-2.

BRITANNICUS: A Play in Two Acts, Adapted from Jean Racine's *Britannicus*. ISBN 978-1-929468-14-0.

BROTHERS ALL: A Play in Three Acts, Based on Dostoyevsky's *The Brothers Karazamov*. ISBN 978-1-929468-11-9.

*ROMANCE OF THE WESTERN CHAMBER —
A MUSICAL*. With Max Lee. Based on S. I. Hsiung's Translation of the Thirteenth-century Chinese Play *Xi Xiang J*i. ISBN 978-1-929468-28-7.

THE GOLEM, MAN OF EARTH: A Play in Two Acts, Based on H. Leivick's *The Golem*. ISBN 978-1-929468-12-6.

THE TROJAN WOMEN: A Play by Euripides Translated from the Greek into English and Adapted in Response to Aristophanes' and Aristotle's Criticism. ISBN 978-1-929468-05-8.

TONY AND CLEO: A Play. ISBN 978-1-929468-13-3.

http://www.granitehillspress.com

www.amazon.com

CONTENTS

To Eternal Friendship
Between the Great Nations of
The People's Republic of China
and
The United States of America

ACKNOWLEDGMENTS

It is a pleasure to acknowledge the people who helped me create *Romance of the Western Chamber–A Musical*:

For the beautiful score, I am grateful to Max Lee, the Hawaii-based composer and arranger, who adapted and arranged traditional Chinese folk tunes that I had selected, composed original music, and scored the work for western instruments.

I thank Louise and Dwight Emery, longtime friends and supporters of all my work, members of the Honolulu Symphony Orchestra and of the Windward Arts Council of Hawaii, for introducing me to Max Lee.

I am indebted to Li-Rong Lilly Cheng, Ph.D., Managing Director, Confucius Institute of San Diego State University, for her multifaceted support of this work. Most notably, Dr. Cheng edited the manuscript, including authenticating the dialect of the characters Hong-niang and Hui, and was the catalyst that realized the premiere of the musical at the Dongpo Theatre, Hangzhou, China, September 9, 2011. In recognition of Dr. Cheng's work on behalf of *Romance of the Western Chamber—A Musical*, she and the Confucius Institute won the Asian Heritage Award 2011 in the Performing Arts.

I thank Kathleen Roche-Tansey, California state coordinator Sister Cities International, leader in American Women for International Understanding, for introducing me to Dr. Cheng.

I thank the major producers of the premiere in China: Professor Wang Baohua (Barbara Wang), Vice-president, College of Music, Zhejiang University of Media and Communications; and Professor Zhimin Wang, Ph.D., Chancellor, Zhejiang University, Hengdian College of Film and Television.

I thank my longtime friend Ingar Quist for help in editing the manuscript.

I am grateful to my wife, Judy, Judith S. Rubenstein, Ed.D., publisher, Granite Hills Press™, for editing all drafts, for helping produce the Chinese premiere, for publishing the work, and for her endless support, wisdom, and love.

THE PREMIERE

Through American and Chinese cooperation, *Romance of the Western Chamber—A Musical* by Howard Rubenstein and Max Lee had its premiere at the Dongpo Theatre, Hangzhou, China, on September 9, 2011. This was the first time a version of the thirteenth-century Chinese play *Xi Xiang Ji* was performed in the English language. The following people were principal participants:

Producers: Dr. Li-Rong Lilly Cheng, Ph.D., Managing Director, Confucius Institute of San Diego State University; Professor Wang Baohua (Barbara Wang), Vice-president, College of Music, Zhejiang University of Media and Communications; Professor Zhimin Wang, Ph.D., Chancellor, Zhejiang University, Hengdian College of Film and Television; and Judith S. Rubenstein, Ed.D., Publisher, Granite Hills Press™. Associate Producers: Hangzhou Municipal Bureau of Culture; Zhejiang Kunqu Opera Theatre; Hangzhou Yue Opera Club; Hangzhou Radio and Television; Dongpo Theatre of Hangzhou.

Director: Jun Kuang. Associate Director: Benjamin Yuan. Assistant Director: Zen Zhong.

Art Director: Bin Zhou; Art Advisor: Barbara Wang.

Music Director: Jun Kuang; Conductor of Orchestra: Clayton Zhan.

Choreographer: Shuling Zhao. Associate Choreographers: Zen Zhong, Zhengying Zhu, Zhehua Yu, Na Ren.

Cast: Tonny Li (Chang Jun-rui); Alicia Zhu (Tsui Ying-ying); Anna Xue (Hong-niang); Barbara Wang (Lady Tsui); Yan Liao (Superior of the Buddhist monastery); Zen Zhong (Flying Tiger); Zach Zhu (General Tu); Andrea Ye (Lord Cheng-heng); Frank Yu (Hui); Ranking Ye (Imperial Messenger).

Dancers: Alice Li, Chengqian Bai, Jiawen Liu, Shang Li, Yang Liu, Shengde Zhang, Guijie Zhao, Jane Zhang, Tina Ji, Diana Qu, Vanessa Yang, Shero He, Sunny Kong, Betty Wang, Rita Zhu, Lisa Liang, Sally Shen, Sara Chen, Joey Yang.

Musicians: Wen Xia, Wenting Sun, Mengjie Ma, Carrey Zhang, Zhao Xia, Angel Zhu, Demi Wang, Xi Yu Wang, Bingqi Zhou.

Stage Manager: Wendy Wu. Assistants to the Stage Manager: Xiaying Niu, Licebirce Li, Caizhi Yang, Kaikai Li, Junhang Lu, Yuqing Chen.

English Tutors: Hongsong Shao, Jinhua Yan.

Props: Haisuo Qiu, Yuan Yuan.

Set Designer: Panpan Lang.

Video Designer: Zhendong Du.

Makeup: Lingying Wang, Yifan Zhang.

Script Editor: Zen Zhong.

Cameramen: Yi Ke, Tianji Tang, Tao Huang, Yan Wang.

Publicist: Wendy Wu.

Mandarin Supertitles: Lusong Jin.

Costume consultant: Barbara Wang.

Howard Rubenstein
San Diego
October 5, 2012

PREFACE

Romance of the Western Chamber–A Musical is based on the Chinese classical play *Xi Xiang Ji*, which tells one of the great love stories of world literature. *Xi Xiang Ji* dates from the thirteenth century, with authorship attributed to Wang Shifu and/or Guan Hanqing. The play was itself based on a twelfth-century "narrative poem of many lyrics" *Hsi-hsiang chu-king-tiao* ("Western Chamber Romance") by Master Tung. This poem in turn was based on a ninth-century short story *Ying-ying Chuan* ("The Story of Ying-ying") by Yuan Chen. I based my version mainly on S. I. Hsiung's "faithful . . . line for line . . . word for word" (Hsiung's words) English translation of *Xi Xiang Ji*, London, Methuen, 1935.

Xi Xiang Ji has held the Chinese stage almost continuously for eight centuries in spite of intermittent condemnations for "obscenity." Its longevity may be attributed to its universality: It is a "rich girl, poor boy" love story. The girl is Tsui Ying-ying, beautiful, intelligent, highly accomplished, and very rich; the boy is Chang Jun-rui, handsome, clever, talented, with literary, musical, and political aspirations, but very poor. When Ying-ying and Jun-rui meet accidentally, it is love at first sight. But insurmountable obstacles, some of which were already in place at the moment of their meeting, impede their love. Ying-ying is betrothed to a man she does not like, let alone love, a rich young official from a distinguished family, but her widowed mother approves the match. Other obstacles arise unexpectedly, and the couple would have no chance of consummating their love and marrying if not for the help of Ying-ying's attendant and devoted friend, Hong-niang, a character that has become so famous in China over the centuries that her name has become synonymous with matchmaker.

The play is remarkably modern, a tribute to the Chinese imperial government that allowed the performing arts to flourish and express authentic human situations and feelings at a time when Europe was in the Dark Ages and produced mostly religious works of art. Although religion plays a role in *Xi Xiang Ji*, it serves only to drive the romantic action of the play and enhance its humanity.

The plot of Rubenstein and Lee's *Romance of the Western Chamber–A Musical* remains faithful to the original, but I have made changes, among them:

I condensed the play from many hours to a few;

I rendered it in standard American English in free verse to make it accessible to an English-speaking audience;

I added music to make it more akin to a Broadway musical, a genre which is popular in both the East and the West. In China, *Xi Xiang Ji* has been transformed several times into operas, but Beijing Opera or one of its variants, although beloved entertainment in China, is appreciated in the West only by aficionados. I wanted the music to have wide appeal to West and East and to be modern while preserving its Chinese origins. To that end, I used as source material the abundant traditional Chinese folk tunes and selected the melodies or melodic phrases that delighted me and were most appropriate to my lyrics. Max Lee adapted and arranged the music and scored it for western instruments while preserving original themes. Where necessary, such as in the ballet and dream sequences, he composed original music in the pentatonic scale to reflect the Chinese influence.

Regarding characters, in the original play, Hong-niang is the same age as Ying-ying; but insofar as youth is not consistent with the character's extraordinary wisdom, common sense, practicality, and effectiveness, I made Hong-niang middle-aged.

Max Lee and I hope that *Romance of the Western Chamber–A Musical* will contribute to building a bridge between the cultures of China and the United States while increasing the friendship between these two great nations, a friendship so essential to world peace. Then he and I, in the words of the play, will have "plucked the flower of success from the moon."

ROMANCE

OF THE

WESTERN CHAMBER

A Musical

CHARACTERS

LADY TSUI, mother of Ying-ying, widow of the late
    prime minister, middle-aged

YING-YING (Tsui Ying-ying), her daughter, late teens

HONG-NIANG, their female servant, middle-aged

CHANG (Mr. Chang, Chang Jun-rui, Jun-ri), scholar and
    poet, early twenties

SUPERIOR, chief monk of the Buddhist monastery,
    middle-aged

FLYING TIGER, leader of the bandits, mid-twenties

HUI, monastery cook, middle-aged

GENERAL TU (also known as General White Horse),
    best friend of Chang, mid-twenties

LORD CHENG-HENG, official, betrothed to Ying-ying,
    late twenties

MESSENGER

IMPERIAL MESSENGER

Soldiers

Bandits

Buddhist Monks

Girls and Women of Ch'ang-an

Dancers and Acrobats

Time: Ninth century during the T'ang Dynasty.

Place: China, Ho-chung Prefecture, the Buddhist monastery; and Ch'ang-an (today called Xian), Imperial Capital of the T'ang Dynasty.

["Overture to Act I"]

ACT I: BEAUTY'S ENCHANTMENT

(China. Ho-chung Prefecture. YING-YING *and* HONG-NIANG *in the garden of the eastern pavilion of the Buddhist monastery.*)

YING-YING: It is late spring—
peach and apricot blossoms everywhere.
Their fragrance fills the air.
Pink and white—how beautiful they are
against the bright blue sky.
They bring a smile to my face,
but a tear to my eye. (*She sings.*)

["The Cruel Wind"]
Many silent sorrows I bear,
but one I have to speak aloud:
When the cruel wind blows the blossoms
off the flowering trees.
(*Humming.*)

Hong-niang, I miss my father so,
Oh, father, you died so soon.
You wouldn't have wanted me to be engaged
to a man I care nothing about.

I will soon be twenty!
The sweet time of my youth
is quickly passing away,
and still I've not found love.

(CHANG *can be heard singing off stage. The road and the Yellow River in front of the monastery is lit up as he enters.* YING-YING *and* HONG-NIANG *hide behind a willow tree.*)

CHANG: (*Sings.*)

["Sail to the Sun, Sail to the Moon"]
Sail to the sun, sail to the moon,
sail to the sun and moon.
I want to embark upon a raft
and sail to the sun and moon.

I'm searching for my love.
I hope to find her soon.
Then we can embark upon my raft
and sail to the sun and to the moon.

Look! That is the Yellow River!
What a magnificent sight it is!
Its source is high in the mountains—
far beyond the clouds reaching to heaven.

It courses and rolls
relentlessly onward
past bridges—those black dragons
crouching on the waves—
until it falls at last into the Eastern Sea.
Oh, that I could embark upon a raft
and sail to the sun and the moon!

SUPERIOR: (*Enters.*) Greetings, young man.
I am the Superior monk of the monastery.
What is your name
and where do you come from?

CHANG: (*Bowing.*) My name is Chang Jun-rui.
My home is Lo-yang, famous for peonies.
I am a poor and starving student.
Even though I'm brilliant,
I've failed the district test
so many times, my examination seat
never grows cold.
And I have no job.
So I wander about, a vagabond, learning as I go.
My destination now is Ch'ang-an, the capital,
to take the imperial exam,
the most important in the land.

To pass that with distinction
assures the best positions.
That is to pluck the flower of success from the moon!

No doubt, kind sir, you will ask,
if I'm so brilliant,
why have I failed the district examination
so many times.
I'll tell you.
My father was Minister of Internal Affairs.
He was a good man and honest.
And so, when he died quite young,
he was penniless.
My mother died shortly thereafter,
while I was still a boy.
I've had to fend for myself ever since.
So I travel about like a leaf in the wind,
and study by light of firefly
or light reflected off snow.
My only desire is to be a bookworm—
to stay put and bore my way
through the ancient classics.
Modern literature does not speak to me at all.
Your monastery is famous.
Would you be so kind as to give me a tour?

SUPERIOR: With pleasure.

(CHANG *and* SUPERIOR *stroll,* SUPERIOR *pointing as they go.*)

There is the Great Hall of Buddha
and there the quarters of the monks.
There is the kitchen.
That is the multitiered pagoda
reaching to the sky.
And there is the western tower
with chambers for visitors.

CHANG: What fine buildings!
(*Pointing to the eastern pavilion.*) But over there!
What place is that?

SUPERIOR: We may not go there.
That is the eastern pavilion,
the private quarters
of the late prime minister Tsui.
His widow, Lady Tsui, lives there
with their daughter, Ying-ying,
and their servant, Hong-niang.

(YING-YING *and* HONG-NIANG *emerge from behind the willow and stroll. As they pass* CHANG, *he smiles at* YING-YING *who returns the smile and exits with* HONG-NIANG.)

CHANG: What a beauty!
I surely knew and loved her
in a previous life! (*Reciting.*)

> Heaven knows how many beauties
> I have seen in my life,
> but none as beautiful as she!
> My soul soars to heaven!
> Or have I found paradise on earth?
> Her every gentle step is so full of grace
> she is like the willow
> in the evening breeze.
> She must be the Goddess
> of the far-off South Seas.
> O what a beauty!

Did you see how she turned and smiled at me?

SUPERIOR: What are you talking about?

(CHANG *gazes deeply into the* SUPERIOR*'s eyes.*)

CHANG: The incredible creature
who fills my heart with yearning.

SUPERIOR: I don't understand.

CHANG: When I look at you—
your head radiating a heavenly glow,
your hair as white as snow,
your face that of a handsome young man—
I know you must have discovered
the secret of eternal youth.

SUPERIOR: I'm still not sure I understand.

CHANG: Your monastery is famous for good deeds,
and I've heard you're hospitable
to poor students.
I've no way of showing
sufficient admiration for you.
Even so, if you'd be so kind
as to put in a good word
to that ravishing beauty,
I'd never ever forget you.

SUPERIOR: Mr. Chang,
surely you have something else to say?

CHANG: Yes, forgive me!
May I rent a room?
I can't afford to pay much.

SUPERIOR: All the western chambers
are vacant, so you can have your pick.
Or, if you prefer, you can share my bed.
There's no charge for a poor student.

CHANG: Your Benevolence is most generous,
but I could not accept the excellent room
where the Reverend Superior lives.
I don't need a chamber with burning incense,
handsome beams, and a southern exposure.
A simple room that faces the eastern pavilion
would suit me fine.

SUPERIOR: A western chamber can easily be arranged.

HONG-NIANG: (*Enters, bows.*)
Most Reverend Superior.
Lady Tsui want know
when going perform prayer
for late prime minister.

(*She smiles and bats eyes flirtatiously at* CHANG.)

CHANG: (*Aside.*) When she was young,
this servant must have been a beauty!
Even though she is the maid,
if only I could sleep with her young mistress,

I'd never ask her to make the bed!
Perhaps she's displaying her charms
to attract the old monk! What a waste!

SUPERIOR: Hong-niang, tell Lady Tsui
that the fifteenth day of the second moon
is the day on which the Buddha receives offerings.
They should come to offer incense
that morning before dawn.

(CHANG *is weeping quietly*.)

SUPERIOR: Mr. Chang, what is the matter?

CHANG: I could not help thinking
of my own departed mother and father.
I was hoping you'd include them in your prayers,
and I'd do my duty as a son
and save their souls.

SUPERIOR: Of course!
I'm sure Lady Tsui will not object.

HONG-NIANG: (*Bowing*.) Venerable Superior,
I must go now.
Mistress wonder what happen to me.

CHANG: (*Bowing before* HONG-NIANG.)
Farewell, lovely lady!

HONG-NIANG: (*Bowing.*)
Ten thousand good wishes on you, kind sir!

CHANG: Are you not Hong-niang,
the attendant of young lady Ying-ying?

HONG-NIANG: I am.

CHANG: If I may be so bold,
I've something to say to you.

HONG-NIANG: Well, then, say it!

CHANG: My name is Chang Jun-rui.
My hometown is Lo-yang.
I am twenty-three years old.
Although intelligent, talented, courteous,
irresistibly handsome, and unsurpassably modest,
I'm still unmarried.

HONG-NIANG: Who ask you?

CHANG: Is your young mistress
in the habit of strolling about out of doors?

HONG-NIANG: What do with you?
Confucius say: "Speak only what proper."
Lady Tsui rule family with iron fist,
and she cold as ice.
And no one—no one!—
come to eastern pavilion without invite.
In future, ask only what proper!

CHANG: Well, then, tell your young mistress
that if her mother is as cold and strict as you say,
her daughter had no right to turn and smile at me
the way she did.
And if I must give up thinking of her,
she must tell me how to do it,
for her image is engraved upon my soul.
Oh, that I could take her in my arms!
Once there, she would never again
care about her ice-cold mother!

(HONG-NIANG *bows and quickly exits*.)

(*To* SUPERIOR.) Your benevolence,
what have you decided
regarding a chamber for me?

SUPERIOR: There is a western chamber
overlooking the garden of the eastern pavilion.
It's a delightful room.
Come, I'll show it to you.

(*Fade-out.*)

(YING-YING *and* HONG-NIANG i*n* *Ying-ying's*
bedroom.)

YING-YING: Did the venerable Superior set the date
for my father's memorial?

HONG-NIANG: Yes. On fifteen day of second moon
offering to Buddha most favorable.
Reverend Superior request
you and mother come before dawn
to burn incense.
But young mistress, have very funny story to tell!
Young student there
when I talk to venerable Superior.
Student say, "Are you not Hong-niang,
maid of young lady Tsui Ying-ying?"
Then he say, "I Chang Jun-rui, from Lo-yang,
twenty-three year old and still unmarried."

YING-YING: (*Shocked and irritated.*) Who told you
to ask such questions?

HONG-NIANG: Not ask! Simply tell!
Then ask if you in habit of going out door.
I tell him, "Not your business!"
and give him good scolding!

YING-YING: (*More irritated.*)
You should not have scolded him!

HONG-NIANG: When man fool, why not scold him?

YING-YING: Have you told this to my mother?

HONG-NIANG: No, not see her.

YING-YING: Good! You must never breathe
a word of this to her! How unexpectedly
love has entered my heart!

(YING-YING *sings*.)

["Bright as the Stars in Heaven"]
He is so beautiful, and when he moves so graceful.
The first time I saw him I could not breathe
and instantly became his.

I keep repeating his name—
Jun-rui, Jun-rui, Jun-rui—
and his face is imprinted on my heart.

His poetry makes me smile or weep,
and shines—how it shines!—
as bright as the stars
and the full radiant moon in heaven.

I keep repeating his name—
Jun-rui, Jun-rui, Jun-rui—
and his face is imprinted on my heart.

Oh, he is so beautiful, and when he moves so graceful.
The first time I saw him I could not breathe
and instantly became his.
I could not breathe and instantly was his!

(*In anguish.*) But I am promised to another!
What am I to do?

(*Fade-out.*)

(*Garden of eastern pavilion.* CHANG *is gazing down from his window.*)

CHANG: How delightful is this western chamber!
From the window, I gaze down
on the garden of the eastern pavilion.
But the night is dark.
O Moon, can you not, for my sake,
come out a little early?

(*The rising moon lights up the garden. He recites.*)

> From the window I gaze on the garden.
> What a beautiful night!
> Midnight and no one's about.
> The moon is bright, and the breeze caressing.
> Skies are clear, not a trace of a cloud.
> The river reflects the silver light of the moon.
> And shadows of trees fall
> and move about the courtyard.

It would be a perfect night
if only she were in sight!
O what a beauty!

(YING-YING *enters the garden with* HONG-NIANG.)

CHANG: There she is!
And more beautiful now than by daylight!
I suspect she entered the garden
just so I could look at her!

YING-YING: (*Lighting the first stick of incense.*)
In burning this first stick of incense,
I pray that my deceased father ascend to heaven.
(*Lighting the second.*)
In burning this second stick,
I pray that my dear mother live ten thousand years.
(*Lighting the third.*)
In burning this third stick, I pray . . .

HONG-NIANG: Yes? Go on!
What you pray?

YING-YING: I pray . . . I pray . . .

HONG-NIANG: Why always get stuck on third stick?
Allow me complete prayer for you:

I pray young mistress find and marry husband
very smart, handsome, and kind,
second to none!

CHANG: (*From his window.*)
I have written a poem to the one I love.
I will recite it from my window
and see what happens.

(*Reciting loudly.*) On this magical night,
when the moon's light is so bright,
I can see the Goddess of the Moon,
who has descended from the sky
into the garden of the eastern pavilion.

YING-YING: Who can that be
who recited such a beautiful poem?

HONG-NIANG: Voice same as foolish student
(*Loudly.*) who twenty-three year old
(*More loudly.*) and still unmarried!

YING-YING: Here is a poem in response to his.

(*Reciting loudly.*) Solitude dwells in the garden.
To no avail the moon's bright light has shone.
Show pity on the girl who sighs there

all alone.
O Moon, why have you come forth
to light up the sky
when my sorrow is so dark?
The one I love is unreal as a mirage—
like the distant horizon
never to be reached.
I cherish him only in my heart,
speak of him only with my lips,
and meet him only in my dreams.

CHANG: (*Overjoyed.*) How prompt
her response! And so apt!
And her voice is sweet as a songbird's!
Now it's my turn.
(*He whistles the tune of* "A Girl So Fair")

YING-YING: Hong-niang, listen!
It is not the sound of wind chimes.
It is a man whistling!
And it's coming from the western chamber!
The music is more powerful
than sabers of warriors on horseback,
more gentle than flower petals falling on water.
The melody expresses the separation of young lovers.

HONG-NIANG: How you know what music express
when no word?

YING-YING: The music says it all.
If he sings the words, you'll see that I'm right.

CHANG: (*Sings.*)

["A Girl So Fair"]
Once there was a lovely girl so fair—
one look, and there's no forgetting her.
When she's out of sight, I am driven to despair.
Oh, that I could join with her forever!
But if I cannot, I will surely die!

YING-YING: How beautiful and yet so sad—
like the weeping of Confucius on seeing the unicorn!
Oh, Hong-niang, go to him and tell him
how much I love the beautiful sadness of the song.

HONG-NIANG: Yes, I go tell him
how much you love song. Only song!

(*Fade-out.*)

(CHANG *in the western chamber.* HONG-NIANG *knocks at the door.*)

CHANG: (*Opening the door.*)
Oh, Hong-niang! I've lost interest in studying.
I haven't touched a book.
I no longer care for advancement or fame.
I am constantly in a daze.
I forget to eat, and I forget to drink,
and I forget what I do or where I go!
I am drunk on love—mad with love.
Love has taken possession of my soul!
(*Abruptly cheerful.*) Did your mistress
like my song?

HONG-NIANG: She like even more
the lips that sing it!

CHANG: I thought so!
I have a letter for her.

(*He hands* HONG-NIANG *the letter.*)

HONG-NIANG: (*Looking at the envelope.*)
How beautiful your handwriting!
Tell me what you write!

CHANG: It says: "What is more precious
than a man's life? So please, lovely lady,
be careful with mine."

HONG-NIANG: How romantic! (*She sings.*)

["Hong-niang's Advice"]
How romantic! How romantic you are!
But dear scholar, who write beautiful poem,
whatever come, always keep career in mind.
The hand that want caress girl
must always be ready
pluck flower of success from moon!
Must not let love entangle
and trip up noble ambition.
Must not for sake of pretty face
fail to attain highest literary honor.
Must not pine away of love.

CHANG: Your words are true,
and I shall carry them always in my heart.
But please deliver my letter!

HONG-NIANG: Only thought day and night
is bring destined match to fulfillment!
So how I not deliver precious letter?
(*Fade-out.*)

(YING-YING *in her bedroom.*)

HONG-NIANG: (*Enters.*) Mr. Chang send letter.

(HONG-NIANG *hands the letter to* YING-YING.)

YING-YING: (*Reads the letter silently, then speaks angrily.*) The audacity!
Am I accustomed to reading such a letter?
How dare you deliver it to me!
I am the daughter of the Prime Minister!
I'm going to tell my mother,
and she'll give you a good thrashing!

HONG-NIANG: Not understand!
You send me to him, and *he* send me back to you!
So why angry at *me?*
Things turning out just as you want,
and suddenly angry! Why? I tell you why!
You suddenly ashame
and want other suffer for what you do!
You not "accustom" to receive such letter!
Who accustom?
Going to tell mother! Tell mother what?
Rather than you tell mother, let me take letter to her
and act like informer!

YING-YING: (*Angrily.*) Against whom
will you be informing?

HONG-NIANG: Against the dumb student,
and he get good thrashing.

YING-YING: Don't be so hasty!
I forgive him—and you, too—but only this once!
But tell me, is he lovesick?

HONG-NIANG: I not tell!

YING-YING: Oh, please tell!

HONG-NIANG: He say when eat, forget eat.
When drink, forget drink.
And when walk, forget where or when stop.

YING-YING: Well, then, a doctor of the highest skill
must be called to examine him!

HONG-NIANG: This not sickness for doctor,
even good one. Patient say on verge of death,
but doctor say in perfect health.
Other disease have remedy, but lovesick no cure—
unless give sickness romantic expression!

YING-YING: How dare you speak of that!
Mr. Chang is like an old friend to me.

HONG-NIANG: More than that, don't you think?
If you afraid flirtation lead to harm
and discover by mother,
no wonder you feel anxious.
In that case, forget him
and care not for his lovesickness!
But let me remind you what you do:
You encourage him climb ladder
you yourself provide;
and now he at dangerous height,
you push ladder away!

YING-YING: But how can he be allowed
to write such a letter?
I shall write him and tell him
not to do it again! (*She writes.*)

HONG-NIANG: But why? Who you fool?

YING-YING: You don't understand!
(*Handing over the note.*) Take this to Mr. Chang!

HONG-NIANG: I refuse take!
In my dream, you two together,
but on waking, you all alone!
That evening when recite poetry,
and he sing to you,
you not consume by passion?
Then did you feel ashame
for that horrible and crazy fellow
as you look so longing at his window?
Suddenly now you ashame
but absolutely refuse to take blame,
and so find fault with another!
But you not fool anyone!
Until now I put up with nonsense.
But no more! (*Contemplating.*)
Now what must I do with letter?
If no deliver, disobey you.
Beside, Mr. Chang expect answer to his letter.
So must deliver yours!

(*Fade-out.*)

(CHANG *in the western chamber.*)

HONG-NIANG: (*Knocks and enters.*)
Romance all over! Finish!

CHANG: Give me her letter!
(*He snatches the letter, reads it rapidly, then smiles.*)
Ah, Hong-niang, today is my lucky day!

HONG-NIANG: What you mean?

CHANG: Your mistress's abuse of me
was all a put-on.

HONG-NIANG: Really? How you know?

CHANG: She says so! Moreover,
she is planning to meet me tonight.

HONG-NIANG: Really? What for?

CHANG: What do you think?

HONG-NIANG: I not believe!

CHANG: You can believe it or not.

HONG-NIANG: Read letter to me!

CHANG: It is a poem of only four lines.

HONG-NIANG: Read it!

CHANG: (*Reads aloud.*)
> When moonlight comes to the western chamber
> and in the garden, shadows fall,
> moving about the pavilion wall,
> then, climb, my precious, climb!

HONG-NIANG: What poem mean?

CHANG: Its meaning is perfectly clear.

HONG-NIANG: Not to me!

CHANG: Then let me explain it:
"When moonlight comes to the western chamber"
means I must wait here until the moon rises,

". . . and in the garden, shadows fall
moving about the pavilion wall"
refers to a designated place in the garden.
Isn't there a tree in the garden
casting shadows on the wall?

HONG-NIANG: Yes, apricot tree.

CHANG: So that must be the place to which I must go.
"Climb, my precious, climb"
means I climb the apricot tree.

HONG-NIANG: And "my precious"?

CHANG: That can be only one person. Me!
The meaning of the poem is perfectly clear!

HONG-NIANG: Why "climb" two time?

CHANG: The second "climb" is poetry—
to complete the line.

HONG-NIANG: *Really?* That what poem mean?

CHANG: Hong-niang, I would never deceive you.
I am a master at solving romantic puzzles!
But I'll read it again.

(*As* CHANG *examines the letter,* YING-YING *appears on her balcony and sings the poem. As* CHANG *begins to read it aloud, the song becomes a duet.*)

YING-YING and CHANG: (*Sing.*)

> ["When Moonlight Comes"]
> When moonlight comes
> to the western chamber
> and in the garden, shadows fall,
> moving about the pavilion wall,
> then climb, my precious, climb!

(*At* YING-YING's *last* "*climb!*" *she and the balcony disappear.*)

CHANG: The message has not changed.

HONG-NIANG: So! Mistress make fool of me!
She very crafty! And she very bold!
She tell you when, where, and how
carry out secret meeting!
To you, she send word so hot
keep one warm in winter,
but to me she speak word so cold
make one freeze in summer!

CHANG: Where is the apricot tree?

HONG-NIANG: Beneath balcony like poem say.
To reach balcony from apricot tree not hard.

CHANG: I know the garden!

HONG-NIANG: Yes, but only through window!
Reciting poetry and singing song
only game.
But mistress' note
show coming of real thing! (*Exits giggling.*)

CHANG: Who could ever have thought
she would give me such hope?
But now I must wait until moonlight!
The wretched day seems endless!
The sun seems glued to the sky!
Move, Sun, move! You have eternity before you,
so why should you care
about shortening one summer day?

(*Fade-out.*)

(HONG-NIANG i*n the garden of the eastern pavilion.*)

HONG-NIANG: To me, young mistress not tell truth,
while in poem to Mr. Chang,
she make secret meeting!

(YING-YING *enters bedroom balcony.*)

How bewitching she look!
Cannot wait to meet lover!
She long to mate with him
like pair of bird—like oriole or swallow!
She restless. She no eat, she no drink.
Only few day ago bashful and shy,
but now so full of passion
can barely control self!

(CHANG *furtively enters the garden.*)

Over there!
I thought it flock of crow casting shadow,
but really handsome scholar hiding behind bush!

(CHANG *steps out and mistaking* HONG-NIANG *for* YING-YING *embraces her.*)

CHANG: Ying-ying, my darling, at last!
I've waited so long for this moment!

HONG-NIANG: (*Vigorously rebuffing him.*)
Oh, you dumb beast! It Hong-niang!
Lucky you make mistake with me!
What if Lady Tsui?

Really must look before hug!
Beside, first must climb apricot tree!

CHANG: I'm sorry, Hong-niang!
I was overly excited.
I'm certain that this evening . . .

HONG-NIANG: Yes? This evening . . . ?

CHANG: I'm going to . . .

HONG-NIANG: Going to . . . ?

CHANG: . . . win her over!

HONG-NIANG: Mr. Chang,
beautiful evening assist you!
But remember, she innocent and young,
so must treat gently and speak soft word.
Now go! End lovesickness!
Climb tree and show man of boldness!

(CHANG *climbs the apricot tree and leaps onto the balcony.*)

YING-YING: (*Frightened.*) Who is it?

CHANG: It's me, Jun-rui!

YING-YING: Oh, Mr. Chang,
what kind of man are you
to suddenly appear on a girl's balcony
at this hour of night?

CHANG: (*Bewildered.*) Uh . . . but . . .
(*Bows head and clasps hands behind back.*)

HONG-NIANG: (*From below, in the garden.*)
Mr. Chang! What become of bold talk?
Why dashing fellow suddenly stop?
Look at him—stand and clasp hand
and bow head, deaf and dumb!
When no one about, tongue wag easy enough.
So! Boldness all make-believe!
Mr. Chang useless as corn tassel
without ear of corn!

YING-YING: Hong-niang, come quickly!
There's a thief on my balcony!

(HONG-NIANG *exits garden.*)

CHANG: Not a thief! Only a poor student!

(HONG-NIANG *enters balcony*.)

YING-YING: I should never have written that note.
It was reckless of me. And I am ashamed.
Now my sole wish is that you restrain yourself!
Mr. Chang, we are like old friends,
so why do you come in secret
like a thief in the night
when I was not expecting you?
Leave my balcony at once!
Hong-niang, I'm going inside. (*Exits*.)

HONG-NIANG: What happen to big talk,
great master of poetic riddle?
Seem *that* riddle you no understand!

CHANG: I did not misunderstand the riddle!
It is your mistress I don't understand!

HONG-NIANG: You let moment escape!
Only pretend bold and amorous!
Well, speak no more of love!
Stop compose seductive poem!
Write no more love letter! No!
Better prepare bachelor life!
Go speak to venerable Superior
about becoming monk!

CHANG: (*Good-natured.*) Hong-niang,
give me a kiss!

(*He pecks her on the cheek.*)

HONG-NIANG: (*Giggling.*) Oh, Mr. Chang,
you crazy man!

(*Fade-out.*)

(SUPERIOR *in the Great hall of Buddha. Early morning
before dawn.*)

    ["Call to Morning Prayers (and Memorial Service)"]

(*Sound of drums and cymbals. MONKS are entering and
sitting.*)

SUPERIOR: This is the fifteenth day
of the second moon,
when the Sakyamuni Buddha entered nirvana.
Those who say prayers today
are sure to gain happiness.
Soon Lady Tsui and her daughter
will come to make sacrifice by burning incense.

(*The Call continues and* MONKS *are still entering.*)

CHANG: (*Enters.*) The sound of drums and cymbals
can be heard in every corner of the monastery.
This is the day of the memorial for my mother and father.
The night is far advanced, and soon it will be dawn.

(*A bell tolls. A* MONK, *a straggler, enters and sits.*)

The ringing of the bell
is the invocation of Buddha.
But my mind is far from religion.
All I can think of is her!
I am aflame with desire!

(CHANG *bows to* SUPERIOR.)

SUPERIOR: Mr. Chang,
it's time for you to make your offering.

CHANG: (*Lights a stick of incense.*)
          May all the living
          enjoy long life on earth!
          And may all the dead
          be happy in paradise!

SUPERIOR: What an excellent prayer!

CHANG: (*Lights a second stick.*)
I pray that the souls of my parents
ascend swiftly to heaven!

SUPERIOR: Another fine prayer!

CHANG: (*Lights a third stick. Speaking softly.*)
I secretly pray
that Hong-niang proves an ally,
that Lady Tsui does not discover
my love for her daughter,
and that when at last I'm alone with her
the dog does not bark!
But most of all, great Buddha,
I pray you help me find the way
to a successful assignation!

SUPERIOR: Mr. Chang, speak up!
I could not hear your last prayer.

(LADY TSUI *enters with* YING-YING *and* HONG-NIANG.)

CHANG: Such overwhelming beauty!
Her face is as white as pear blossoms,
her figure as lissome as the willow,
her fragrance like mandarin oranges.
She is pure enchantment!

SUPERIOR: Lady Tsui, I have a favor to ask.
Scholar Chang is a visitor.
After his parents died, he had no opportunity
to show filial gratitude,
so he asked me to include them
in this morning's memorial ceremony.
I promised I would
without consulting you.
I hope you don't mind.

LADY TSUI: Mind? Why should I mind
when he's acted so nobly?

CHANG: The venerable Superior,
though advanced in years,
can't keep his eyes off Ying-ying!
To think even a head monk can behave like a fool!

SUPERIOR: Lady Tsui and Ying-ying!
It is time for you to burn incense.

(LADY TSUI *and* YING-YING *light a stick of incense, but* YING-YING *does not take her eyes off* CHANG.)

["Early Morning Memorial Service"]

MONKS: (*Chanting in Sanskrit.*) *Namo Amito-fo. Namo Amito-fo.*

Boundless light and boundless life is the Buddha.
Boundless light and boundless life gives the Buddha.

YING-YING: (*Speaking to herself, above the chanting.*)
Oh, I love him so!

LADY TSUI: (*Sharply.*)
Hush until the prayers are over!

MONKS: *Namo Amito-fo, Namo Amito-fo.*
Boundless light and boundless life is the Buddha.

SUPERIOR: (*After the chanting ends.*)
With the rising of the sun,
the memorial ceremony is over.
All may return to their quarters.

(ALL *depart except* YING-YING *and* CHANG, *who, on opposite sides of the stage, gaze longingly at each other and sing.*)

["Only a Dream"]

YING-YING:

  Why do I
  dishonor the Buddha
  and my father?
  Is it real what I feel
  or only a dream?
  In spite of myself,
  I keep repeating his name,
  and his face is imprinted
  on my heart.
  Where is the dutiful child?
  What is happening to me?
  Is it real what I feel?
  Or is it just a dream? Ah!

CHANG:

  I should be a good son,
  so why have I lost
  my sense of duty?
  Is it real what I feel
  or is it just a dream?
  In spite of myself,
  I keep repeating her name,
  and her face is imprinted
  on my heart.
  Where is the dutiful child?
  What is happening to me?
  Is it real what I feel?
  Or is it just a dream? Ah!

(*As* YING-YING *and* CHANG *sing, they draw ever closer so that by the end of the duet, they are about to touch.   At the critical moment, the* SUPERIOR *and* HONG-NIANG *enter from opposite sides.*)

SUPERIOR: (*Sternly.*) Children, prayers are over!
Return to your quarters at once!

HONG-NIANG: (*Sternly.*) Ying-ying,
mother want see you!

(*Fade-out.*)

(*Outside the monastery.*)

["The Bandits Dance"]

(*Sudden sound of rolling drums, clashing gongs, and shouting as* FLYING TIGER *enters with* BANDITS *brandishing swords and performing a frightening, militaristic ballet.   When the ballet ends,* FLYING TIGER *speaks.*)

FLYING TIGER: (*Arrogantly.*) I am Flying Tiger,
the most famous of bandits.
I command five thousand men.
We've come for the girl Tsui Ying-ying,
daughter of the Prime Minister.
Now that's a prize worth winning!
I've heard she has overwhelming charms—

beautiful eyes, a winning smile, a dancer's grace,
and a face as lovely as the lotus in springtime.
I intend to take her and make her my wife!
(*To his* BANDITS.) Men, capture Tsui Ying-ying!

(FLYING TIGER *and* BANDITS *exit shouting
accompanied by drums, cymbals, and gongs*.)

(*Fade-out*.)

(*Monastery courtyard.   Shouts of the bandits and the
sounds of the gongs and drums can still be heard*.)

LADY TSUI: (*Enters*.) What is going on?
What is all that noise?

SUPERIOR: (*Enters, agitated.*)
Calamity! Great calamity!
Flying Tiger and his five thousand bandits
have completely surrounded the monastery
as tight as iron hoops around a barrel!
They want to kidnap Ying-ying
and make her Flying Tiger's wife.

LADY TSUI: Flying Tiger is a hero's name.
He doesn't sound heroic to me.

YING-YING: (*Enters.*) What's happening?
What's all that racket?

LADY TSUI: Flying Tiger
with his five thousand bandits
have surrounded the monastery.
He intends to make you his wife!

YING-YING: But he has never even seen me!

LADY TSUI: But he's heard about you:
"overwhelming charms . . . beautiful eyes . . .
winning smile . . . dancer's grace . . .
a face as lovely as the lotus in springtime."

YING-YING: Oh, what is to be done?
There's no way to escape
and no place to hide!
Listen to the beating of the drums!
And see all the dust
from the thundering hooves of the horses
rising in clouds to eclipse the sun!
We'll all be killed!
What does he care about this monastery

and that it was built through gifts from my father?
And so, after he kills us all,
he will burn the buildings to the ground!

LADY TSUI: Death for me
would not be premature,
but you, dear child, are not yet married!

YING-YING: It's best
to hand me over to the bandits
so that your lives will be spared,
and the monastery not reduced to ashes.

LADY TSUI: That is very noble,
but how can a mother hand her daughter
over to a bandit?

YING-YING: In that case,
it's best for me to hang myself!

LADY TSUI: That is out of the question
when you have no husband!

YING-YING: Well, then, what if I marry
the person who drives off the bandits?

LADY TSUI: An excellent idea!
(*Loudly to* ALL.) Attention, attention!
To anyone who devises a plan
to drive off the bandits,
I will give Ying-ying as his bride.
Whoever he turns out to be,
he's got to be better than Flying Tiger!

CHANG: I have such a plan!

YING-YING: Mr. Chang has a plan!

LADY TSUI: (*Ignoring her.*) To anyone
who drives off the bandits,
I'll give Ying-ying as his wife.

CHANG: (*Loudly.*) I have such a plan!
It requires the help of the beneficent Superior.

SUPERIOR: Mr. Chang, I am not a fighting man.
I think you need to select another.

CHANG: Don't worry!
Fighting won't be necessary.
All you have to do is go out
and deliver the following speech.
You say:

"Honorable Flying Tiger,
Ying-ying's mother wishes to remind you
that her daughter is in mourning for her father.
If you wish to marry her,
you must show respect
to your dead future father-in-law.
So, you must withdraw
to a distance of one arrow's flight
from the monastery
and wait there for three days
until the religious rites
for your dead future father-in-law,
are over.
At the end of the three days,
Lady Tsui assures you,
her daughter will become your bride.
Your future mother-in-law says
if you deny her request,
you will bring bad luck on your worthy self
and on all your brave soldiers."

Most venerable Superior, that is the speech.
Flying Tiger will listen,
and if he has any sense, he will obey.

SUPERIOR: I'll do it.
But what happens after three days?

CHANG: My friend General Tu,
also known as General White Horse,
is commander of the soldiers
guarding the nearby mountain pass.
He is an invincible warrior.
He and I are blood brothers,
and if I write to him, he will come to our rescue.

SUPERIOR: His reputation is well known,
and I am confident he will save us.
Now I'm going to deliver the speech.

(*The drums of the* BANDITS *have become very loud,
but as soon as the* SUPERIOR *exits, they become silent.*)

YING-YING: All the monks
are only thinking of ways to save themselves.
Who cares at all for my mother or me,
except you, Mr. Chang?
This is not a case of a scholar
wishing to show off how much he knows.
This is a case of a man whose advice is real.
Success or failure depends entirely on his plan,
and his plan hinges on a letter.
With the point of a pen, he intends to sweep away
five thousand ruthless bandits!

SUPERIOR: (*Returning.*) All went well!
Flying Tiger agreed to Lady Tsui's terms.
He sends her his highest regards,
and assures her how lucky she is to get him
for a son-in-law!
But he strictly limits us to three days.
If Ying-ying does not come to him by then,
he will kill us all.
Mr. Chang, write your letter to General Tu
without delay!

CHANG: I've already written it! (*Holding letter up.*)
All we need is someone to deliver it!

SUPERIOR: The cook in the kitchen . . .
his name is Hui.
He's studying to be a monk,
but he's fierce and enjoys slaying dragons!
He's really the only one
who can do the job.
But he's stubborn. Let's see what I can do.
(*In a loud voice.*) I have a dangerous mission,
and I don't know who to send.
Who is brave enough to go?

HUI: (*Enters.*) Who called?

SUPERIOR: I have a dangerous mission.
I have a letter that must go immediately
to General White Horse.

HUI: Only one man to send
on dangerous mission. Me!

SUPERIOR: It will take you out of the kitchen
and away from your prayers.

HUI: I glad get out of kitchen
and no believe in prayer.
Sacred book boring,
and I not believe in repentance.
Worship not right job for me!
What I want is enter tiger den
and slay all tiger!
But now I have letter to deliver!
Where is it?

(CHANG *hands letter to* HUI.)

CHANG: Do you want to go alone
or with other monks?

HUI: You want send me
with young monk carrying parasol?
No! I much rather go alone!

CHANG: And if the bandits stop you,
what then?

HUI: I bow and say,
"Honorable gentlemen,
I humble monastery cook
on way to market to order food
for exalted Flying Tiger wedding banquet!"

CHANG: (*Laughing.*) Excellent!
When can you start?

HUI: If only you stop talking,
I already on my way!
I, your hero, now off
to bring White Horse General from heaven!

(*As* HUI *runs off, fade-out.*)

(FLYING TIGER *and* BANDITS *outside the monastery.*)

FLYING TIGER: (*Shouting.*) General Tu is coming
with banners flying! Men! Prepare to fight!

["Triumphal Entrance of General Tu"]

(*General* TU *and* SOLDIERS *march in, banners flying.
Face to face with* FLYING TIGER *and* BANDITS, *they
halt. Both sides momentarily size each other up.*)

["The Battle"]

[*Both sides suddenly engage in a fierce battle dance with
sabers. At the end,* TU *captures* FLYING TIGER *and
hands him over to two of his men, who exit with him.*]

TU: I order your leader—what's his name?—
(*Sarcastically.*) "Slithering Snake"?
Flying Tiger!—executed.
As for the rest of you,
those who do not wish to continue as soldiers
may return to your homes and farms.
And those who wish to rejoin the army
may reenlist and join my troops.

(CHANG *enters. TU and* CHANG *bow to each other.*)

CHANG: General Tu, when I saw you
and your men approaching,
it was like stars pouring forth from the Milky Way!

TU: I came as quickly as I could.
I'm glad to see you, brother!

(*The two embrace. Then the* SUPERIOR, LADY TSUI,
YING-YING, *and* HONG-NIANG *enter.* TU *and*
CHANG *bow to them.*)

SUPERIOR: General White Horse,
I am the Superior of the monastery.
Everyone here is forever indebted to you.
(*Bowing.*) One thousand thanks, sir!

LADY TSUI: General White Horse,
I am Lady Tsui, the widow of the late prime minister.
For saving our lives, (*Bowing.*) ten thousand thanks, sir.

YING-YING: I am Ying-ying, Lady Tsui's daughter.
For saving the monastery,
(*Bowing.*) ten thousand thousand thanks, sir.

TU: The crisis is over, so you need not thank me.
Besides, I was only doing my duty.

(TU *admires* YING-YING, *then grins and winks at* CHANG.)

Mr. Chang,
What kept you at the monastery
rather than coming to visit me?

CHANG: My journey from home
was so exhausting,
I had to rest here.
Today I'd gladly accompany you
to your headquarters,
but Lady Tsui just promised
her daughter to me in marriage.
When the date is set,
I'd like you to do me the honor
of being my best man.

TU: It is I who am honored.
Congratulations, younger brother,
on catching such a beauty!
But as Flying Tiger's bandits have just surrendered,
I must deal with them.
So, to all I say, farewell!

ALL: Farewell, General!

["Triumphal Exit of General Tu"]

(TU *and* SOLDIERS *exit, banners flying, with bound* BANDITS. *All others exit except* HONG-NIANG *and* CHANG.)

HONG-NIANG: And so five thousand bandit
led by five thousand soldier
drift away like floating cloud.
To you, Mr. Chang, we show
greatest appreciation and admiration.
(*Aside.*) How handsome he is and smart!
Could not fail touch Ying-ying heart!
(*To* CHANG.) Oh, Mr. Chang, I almost forget.
Lady Tsui invite you banquet at eastern pavilion.

CHANG: Tell Lady Tsui I accept!

HONG-NIANG: No student ever turn down
dinner invitation!

CHANG: Are there going to be other guests?

HONG-NIANG: No. Lady Tsui invite only you
to thank and announce Ying-ying betrothal.
Lady Tsui expect you soon! (*Exits.*)

CHANG: Oh, Flying Tiger,
you are my great benefactor!
I owe everything to you!
I will ask the benevolent Superior
to perform a memorial to save your soul.
For it is my sincerest wish
that Flying Tiger fly straight to paradise!

CHANG: (*With his fingers he combs his hair, and with his hands he brushes his clothing. He beams, and runs out shouting.*) A banquet! For me!

(*Fade-out.*)

(*In the eastern pavilion dining room,* LADY TSUI *is sitting at a small table set for four.*)

HONG-NIANG: (*Enters and stands aside.*)
Mr. Chang coming, my Lady.

CHANG: (*Enters and bows.*) Good evening, Lady Tsui.

LADY TSUI: Please be seated, Mr. Chang.

(*She points to the seat at the head of the table, and*
CHANG *sits.*)

If it had not been for you, Mr. Chang,
we would not be alive today.
So I have prepared a small supper,
which in no way adequately repays you
for all that you have done.

CHANG: The bandit's defeat is a thing of the past
and not worth mentioning.

YING-YING: (*Enters.*) Mother, this is an occasion
that calls for a great celebration.
Why, then, is it so spare?
It's not because you don't have enough money
for an elaborate affair.
And why, when we're celebrating two events—
one in gratitude to Mr. Chang for saving our lives
and the second in honor of my engagement to him—
is there only one meal?

LADY TSUI: Come here, my daughter,
sit down (*Pointing to the seat between herself and*
CHANG.) and pay your respects to your elder brother.

CHANG: I do not like those words.

YING-YING: (*Sitting.*) Oh, my mother
is going back on her word!
Mother, why do you call Mr. Chang "elder brother"?

LADY TSUI: Hong-niang,
fill elder brother's cup with wine.

(HONG-NIANG *starts to fill* CHANG*'s cup, but he stops
her with his hand.*)

CHANG: (*Sullen.*) I don't drink.

YING-YING: (*Aside.*) Who could have thought
that my happiness was dissolving into nothingness?
My beloved is like a man standing on a bridge
awaiting his lover, when unexpectedly
a giant wave washes over the bridge
and sweeps him off in the torrent.

LADY TSUI: My daughter,
fill your elder brother's cup!

(YING-YING *starts to fill* CHANG*'s cup.*)

CHANG: I've already said I don't drink.

YING-YING: (*Offering the cup*.) Mr. Chang,
please take my advice and drink some wine.
When it begins to take effect,
it will ease the pain.

(CHANG *drinks in large gulps*. YING-YING *sings*.)

["O Sorrow!"]
O Sorrow! My sorrow
is deeper than the deepest sea
and vaster than the sky.
From the moment I first saw him,
I could not help thinking
he was the Spirit of the Magic Mountain
or the God of the Enchanted Sea.
O Sorrow! How cruel to lose him now!

The light in my heart has gone out.
How cruel my mother is—
she has destroyed a future
that promised so much happiness.
She tricked him!
When she needed him, she made him a promise
she never intended to keep.
And now she is getting rid of him
by calling him my "elder brother."

LADY TSUI: Hong-niang,
conduct Ying-ying to her room.

(YING-YING *and* HONG-NIANG *exit.*)

CHANG: (*Standing and bowing.*) Lady Tsui,
I must go, too. But before I do,
I must tell you what's on my mind.
When the bandits were about to attack us,
did you not say, "To anyone who devises a plan
to drive them off, I'll give Ying-ying as wife"?
Were those not your very words?

LADY TSUI: They were.

CHANG: And who was it
who came forth with a plan?

LADY TSUI: You, sir,
and it is to you we owe our lives.
I would never deny it.

CHANG: So why
do you suddenly call me "elder brother"?

LADY TSUI: Mr. Chang,
I understand your disappointment.
But when the late prime minister was alive,
he betrothed my daughter to another,
to Lord Cheng-heng.
So what am I to do? I cannot go against
my late husband's wishes.

CHANG: Lord Cheng-heng?

LADY TSUI: Yes, do you know him?

CHANG: If he's the one I know . . .

LADY TSUI: Yes?

CHANG: No. Forget it! It can't be the same man,
not if Ying-ying's engaged to him.

LADY TSUI: Mr. Chang, I have decided to reward you
with a great sum of money,
and I hope you select some other young woman
worthy of you.
This seems to me the best solution.

CHANG: Do you really think so?
Supposing Flying Tiger had carried out
his intentions?
What would you have said then?
Do you really think I would take your money?
Lady Tsui, I was filled with joy
when you led me to believe
your daughter and I would marry.
But now you have changed your mind
and expect to buy me off.
I was under the impression
your word was as good as gold,
but I see I was mistaken.
Good night, Lady Tsui.

(CHANG *bows and exits.*)

(*Fade-out.*)

(YING-YING *is in her bedroom.* HONG-NIANG *enters.*)

YING-YING: The venerable Superior sent me a message
saying Mr. Chang was very ill,
so I've written him a note.

HONG-NIANG: If your mother find out,
she no like.

YING-YING: My mother cares nothing for my
happiness.
Deliver this note to Scholar Chang.
It contains a prescription to cure him!

HONG-NIANG: Oh, Mistress,
no medicine cure broken heart.

YING-YING: Deliver this note.

HONG-NIANG: Mr. Chang's sickness serious
not only because of mother,
but also because of you!
Other night you hurt him with icy word.
All could go well, but you broke spell
by talking nonsense, saying, "Mr. Chang,
you old friend,
so why you come like thief in night?"
I know you not speak truth!
Cannot blame mother for that!
Now you say, "Mr. Chang,
I have prescription to cure you."
Mistress, false hope far worse than no hope at all.

YING-YING: Hong-niang, deliver my note!

(*Fade-out.*)

(CHANG *in western chamber. A knock at the door.*)

CHANG: Enter!

(HONG-NIANG *enters.*)

HONG-NIANG: Mr. Chang, how you feel?

CHANG: How do I feel? I feel like hanging myself!

HONG-NIANG: What good that do?
Beside, no need for drastic measure.
My mistress send excellent prescription.

CHANG: Let me see it!

(*She hands him the note. He reads it and smiles.*)

It is a poem of only two lines,
but my sickness has been instantly cured!

HONG-NIANG: Read short poem to me!

CHANG: :
>   Tonight, my love, without fail,
>   I will come to you.

HONG-NIANG: Oh, this time no riddle!
I understand every word!

CHANG: (Sings.)

> [Reprise: "Bright as the Stars of Heaven"]
> She is so beautiful, and when she moves so graceful.
>   The first time I saw her I could not breathe
>   and instantly became hers.
>
>   I keep repeating her name—
>   Ying-ying, Ying-ying, Ying-ying—
>   and her face is imprinted on my heart.
>
> Oh, she is so beautiful, and when she moves so graceful.
>   The first time I saw her I could not breathe
>   and instantly became hers.
>   I could not breathe and instantly was hers!

HONG-NIANG: But I wonder, she really coming?
(*Considering. Shaking her head.*) Not coming!

CHANG: Hong-niang, don't trouble yourself
with wondering!
All I expect from you is to do your best for me.

HONG-NIANG: Mr. Chang,
I never do but best for you.

["I Never Do But Best For You"]
I never do but best for you,
and do not do in hope reward.
I not expect jade ring or gold bling or necklace,
precious bracelet, Oh, no!
Only want simple thing, small thing—
nice floral crown,
embroidered gown reaching to ground.
With thought of that she come to you tonight. Oh, yes!

But, Mr. Chang, I want you do your part!
Remember, success or failure depend entirely on you!

(*Fade-out.*)

(CHANG *in western chamber*.)

CHANG: Why isn't she here yet?
Is she ever going to come?
(*He sings*.)

> ["Waiting Expectantly"]
> Suspense fills the western chamber
> as the crows caw in the courtyard
>   and the gentle wind dances
>   through the rustling bamboo.
>
> His loving heart is wildly beating,
>   and he thinks if she won't come,
>   all hope will disappear
>   like a stone into the deep.
>
> Suspense fills the western chamber
> as the crows caw in the courtyard
>   and the gentle wind dances
>   through the rustling bamboo.

Is it fair that I'm so in love with her?
Is there a medicine I can take to make me forget her?

(*Knock at the door*.)

HONG-NIANG: (*Excitedly.*) It Hong-niang
with young mistress!

CHANG: (*Opening the door. HONG-NIANG shoves
YING-YING into the room.*)

HONG-NIANG: Go in! That right!
I wait for you outside. (*Closing the door.*)

(CHANG *and* YING-YING *look lovingly at each other.
He leads her into the room. After a moment, he kisses
her tenderly.*)

CHANG and YING-YING: (*Singing.*)

> [Reprise: "When Moonlight Comes"]
> When moonlight comes to the western chamber
> and in the garden shadows fall
> moving about the pavilion wall,
> then climb, my precious, climb!

(CHANG *takes* YING-YING *into his arms and they kiss
passionately.*)

(*Fade-out accompanied by* ["Act I Fade-out Music"].)

INTERMISSION

["Overture to Act II"]

ACT II: THE PARTING

(YING-YING *and* CHANG *are making final adjustments to their clothing; he helps her adjust her gown; then both step into their slippers. They look lovingly at each other.*)

CHANG: You are the most beautiful creature
I've ever laid eyes on!
And I love you with all my heart and soul!

(CHANG *takes hold of* YING-YING's *hands while gazing at her.*)

CHANG: (*Sings.*)

["Sailed to the Sun"]
Sailed to the sun, sailed to the moon,
I've sailed to the sun and moon.
I have embarked upon my raft
and sailed to the sun and moon.
I found my love
right here in my little room,
my own true love
right here in my little room.

YING-YING: (*Joins* CHANG *in duet.*)

> Sailed to the sun, sailed to the moon,
> We've sailed to the sun and moon.
> We have embarked upon our raft
> and sailed to the sun and moon.
> Yes, we've sailed to the sun and moon!

(*They kiss tenderly. Monastery bell tolls, followed by knock at the door.*)

HONG-NIANG: (*Enters.*) Bell toll, dawn come.
Must go so Lady Tsui not miss us.

CHANG: But tell me, my love,
when shall we meet here again?

HONG-NIANG: Must go now!

(YING-YING *and* HONG-NIANG *exit;* YING-YING *turns and smiles at him.* CHANG *looks longingly after her, then slowly closes the door.*)

CHANG: Was it all a dream?
It was no dream. She was so soft and warm,
and her fragrance fills the air—peonies!
Oh, how I miss her already!

(*His mood changes.*) And yet,
what about the imperial examination?
And when do I leave for the capital?
(*He sings.*)

> ["The Morning Star Is Rising"]
> The morning star is rising
> and the dawn is breaking. (*Humming.*)
> I must prepare for the next stage
> of my journey.
> I hear the happy sound of rippling water.
> Clouds roll by. I feel so alone.
> Oh, how I miss my dear beloved now!

(*His mood reverts.*)
Oh, I hope she comes again soon—
maybe this afternoon!

(*Fade-out.*)

(HONG-NIANG *in the garden of the eastern pavilion.*)

HONG-NIANG: If she only continue
go at moonlight and return with morning star,
great joy go on and on.
But could not wait, grew too bold,
and took chance any time of day.
Lady Tsui very clever
and make something out of nothing.
So she suspect something.
May even suspect
lowly maid Hong-niang arrange this!
Ying-ying has new radiance.
She quite different from before.
Lady Tsui must notice.
She soon take me aside and say,
"Oh, you nasty woman!
I order you watch over my daughter—
but instead you lead astray!"

LADY TSUI: (*Enters angrily.*)
Oh, you nasty woman!
I ordered you to watch over my daughter—
but instead you lead her astray!
Do you confess?

HONG-NIANG: Lady Tsui, nothing to confess!
When we learn elder brother sick,
we visit him to ask about him.

LADY TSUI: Sick? Visit? Ask?
And what did he say?

HONG-NIANG: He say,
Lady Tsui return good with evil,
so joy turn to sadness, and that why he sick.
Then he let me go,
but ask Ying-ying stay behind.

LADY TSUI: An unmarried girl left behind,
all alone with a young man!

HONG-NIANG: Yes, to try acupuncture
or moxibustion!
But how I know it end
in mating like nightingale or swallow?
Young couple keep company ever since.
Surely you not want detail!
Now they devote to each other
and happy in heart and soul!
Better forgive small offense.
When jade polisher find tiny flaw in jade,
no remove for fear of making worse.

Best now let couple marry.
Beside, very good match.

LADY TSUI: Now I understand!
You arranged this! You are wicked!
Hong-niang, go and tell Ying-ying
and that animal I want to see them. Now!

HONG-NIANG: (*Calling*.) Mistress Ying-ying!
Mother want see you! Now!
And Mr. Chang, Lady Tsui want see you, too! Now!
Your affair discover!

(YING-YING *and* CHANG *enter sheepishly.*   LADY
TSUI *scowls at them and sings*.)

["Lady Tsui's Discovery"]
Ying-ying! Daughter! Innocent, precious flower!
Daughter! Ying-ying!
Now is your most shameful hour.
Chang, you scoundrel! No scholar as you claim!
Ha! Villain! Liar!
I'll report you and your game.
But to expose this shame
would tarnish and soil our good name.
Our family honor all depends on her.
How can I right things again?

YING-YING: (*Sings.*)
Mother! Mother! Sorry I've brought you shame.
Mother, it's all my fault! I should have known better.
Please don't blame her. She did nothing wrong.
Mother, it's all my fault!

CHANG: (*Sings.*)
No! That's not true! I am the one to blame.
No, no, it's all my fault! I shouldn't have let her.
Hong-niang knew our love was truly strong.
No, no, it's all my fault! I shouldn't have let her.

HONG-NIANG: (*Sings.*)
Well, not my fault!

LADY TSUI: (*Sings.*)
Hong-niang! Worthless! You failed to take good care.
Protect her from danger. Instead you led her right there!
I should have never let him near.
He brought to life my deepest fear.

HONG-NIANG: (*Sings.*)
Wait! Lady Tusi, all your fault!

LADY TSUI: (*Sings.*)
Mine?! Mine?! How can you say that?!

HONG-NIANG: (*Sings.*)
You say one who save our life
can take Ying-ying as sweet wife.
You break promise. No! Not right.
So no other choice in sight.
Chang must marry Ying-ying now,
save fam'ly name.
You must allow.

LADY TUSI: (*Sings.*)
How dare you, lowly servant, speak to me as you do!
And yet, I know that all you say is true.
So, in the end, I must give my daughter to that brute!

LADY TSUI: Mr. Chang, I have no choice
but to let my daughter marry you,
even though our family has never had a son-in-law
without a good position.
So you must proceed to the capital at once
and take the imperial examination.
If you pass with honors
and get an outstanding appointment,
you may return and marry my daughter.
But if you fail, don't bother! (*Storms out.*)

CHANG: Ying-ying, beloved,
I shall return in triumph

to the tune of flutes and drums.
And Hong-niang,
I'll bring you a crown of flowers
and a beautiful embroidered gown
reaching to the ground

(*Fade-out.*)

(YING-YING *and* HONG-NIANG *in the monastery
courtyard.*)

YING-YING: Separation is the saddest thing in life.
Where will he sleep tonight?
Will I find him in my dreams? (*Sings.*)

["Bitter Is the Wind"]
As the wild geese fly from north to south
and the autumn leaves scatter,
bitter is the wind.
Oh, why did we meet so late
and now must part so soon?
O Autumn Sky,
please slow the setting of the sun
and departure of my love!
Bitter is the wind.

(LADY TSUI *enters from one side, and* CHANG, *valise in hand, enters from the opposite. He puts down the valise.*)

LADY TSUI: Mr. Chang, I have promised my daughter to you in marriage,
so you must prove yourself worthy.

(SUPERIOR *enters, and* ALL *bow.*)

SUPERIOR: Mr. Chang,
the time has come to say good-bye.

LADY TSUI: Mr. Chang,
I hope you always keep in mind
the desirability of securing the highest grade.

YING-YING: No matter what your grade,
come back to me soon, my beloved!
At the capital the weather will be cold.
Take care of yourself, my precious!
Dress warm!
Be sure to always get a good night's sleep!
Oh, to whom will I tell my cares and sorrows?
Heaven cares nothing for human suffering.
(*Sings.*)

["If the Yellow River Runs Dry"]
If the Yellow River runs dry while you are away,
my tears will make it overflow.
And when night falls on the western chamber,
I will gaze there with sadness
as I watch the moon rise.
I'll wait for you forever!

Oh, my dearest, promise you won't fall in love
with another!

CHANG: Darling, all I want in life
is to share the same bed with you,
and in death always to share the same grave.
I already miss you so!

HONG-NIANG: No time talk lowly grave!
Time think high exam'nation grade—
pluck flower success from moon!

SUPERIOR: Mr. Chang, study hard
during the next six months,
and you will easily pass the spring examination.
Here is some money to help pay expenses.

CHANG: Most reverend Superior,
how can I ever thank you? How shall I ever repay you?

SUPERIOR: By passing,
and obtaining a worthy position.

CHANG: I'll do my best.
Ten thousand thousand thanks! (*Bows*.)

(CHANG *embraces* YING-YING. SUPERIOR *hands* CHANG *his valise. After one last look at* YING-YING, CHANG *exits*.)

YING-YING: (*Searching with longing after him, then singing*.)

> ["Thick Woods and Evening Mist"]
> Thick woods and evening mist
> and the setting sun
> so soon, so soon hide him from view.
> All nature seems to bear me a grudge.
> Without him what will I do?
> May the Goddess of Mercy protect him,
> protect him from harm.

SUPERIOR: Let us return to our quarters.

(*Fade-out accompanied by* ["Act II Fade-out Music"].)

["Intermezzo"]

ACT III: THE HOMECOMING

(YING-YING *in her bedroom.*)

YING-YING: It's been six months
since my beloved left for the capital.
My thoughts are always of him.   (*She gazes out the
window and sings.*)

["A Lonely Boat"]
I enter my room and gaze out the window
toward the towering green hills.
The trees are enveloped in mist.
And on the river a lonely boat waits at the dock,
while in her bedroom
a lonely girl waits for her love.

HONG-NIANG: (*Enters, letter in hand, with great
excitement.*) Mistress! Mistress!
Letter just arrive for you!

(HONG-NIANG *hands the letter to* YING-YING.)

YING-YING: (*Opening the letter and reading it aloud in
excitement.*)

It is from Chang Jun-rui! He writes:

"Dearest Ying-ying,
I have just learned
of my great good fortune!
I passed the imperial examination with high honors,
and am among the top three!
I have only to wait for my official assignment.
Tonight I will be a guest
at the imperial banquet
in honor of the successful candidates.
As soon as the emperor permits, I will return to you.
From your Jun-rui."

HONG-NIANG: Oh, mistress dear! Congratulation!

(YING-YING *runs to her desk, opens a drawer, and produces a small package.*)

I knew this was going to happen!
I've already written him a congratulatory note
and enclosed a small gift.
Hong-niang, run and dispatch this parcel!
And tell the messenger to tell Mr. Chang . . .

HONG-NIANG: Yes? What I tell messenger?

YING-YING: Tell the messenger
to be sure to tell Mr. Chang . . .

HONG-NIANG: Yes? Yes! Speak up!
What must tell him?

YING-YING: Tell the messenger
to tell him . . . I love him!

(*Fade-out.*)

(CHANG *in his room in* Ch'ang-an, *the capital.*)

CHANG: After passing the examination,
I expected to leave the capital at once,
but quite unexpectedly
the Grand Chancellor's daughter
has fallen in love with me and wants to marry me,
and her father not only approves
but insists on it!
Moreover, also unexpectedly,
I received an offer of a professorship
in the Department of Chinese Literature
here at the Imperial University!
What a dilemma! What should I do?
Well, Ying-ying is betrothed to Lord Cheng-heng. . . .

(CHANG *freezes, as if cast under a spell.*)

["Temptation Reverie"]

(*Young women appear, and* CHANG *unfreezes. The women dance seductively, all the while tempting him to go off with them. He joins in the dance but resists their advances until the end, when he is about to go off with one, the Grand Chancellor's daughter. Suddenly, there is a flash of lightning followed by a clap of thunder, whereupon the women vanish and* CHANG *snaps out of it.*)

MESSENGER: (*Enters.*) Mr. Chang?

CHANG: Yes.

MESSENGER: I am a messenger with a small package for you.

(CHANG *takes the package, opens it, removes the letter and reads.*)

CHANG: "Jun-rui, my love,
your Ying-ying sends many congratulations!
Oh, my beloved, how I miss you!
I send you a small gift of a jade ring,
a symbol of our love.

(*He holds up the ring and admires it, then places it on his finger.*)

"I also send you a poem.
The poem's title is 'The Causes of Joy and Sorrow.'
        Joy has many causes,
        but the feeling of Joy is always the same.
        And Sorrow has many causes,
        but the feeling of Sorrow is ever the same.
        How strange that tears follow both Joy and
                Sorrow.
        So limited are human feelings,
        except my boundless love for you!"

What a beautiful poem—and so full of wisdom!
I've known many intelligent women in my lifetime,
but none as intelligent as she.
Wait! She adds a postscript:

"Spring winds are very piercing,
so be sure to dress warm.
I can't wait to see you again.
Your Ying-ying."

How romantic my Ying-ying is,
second to none! How could I even think of another!
I will regard the jade ring as a good-luck charm
and the poem as precious
as a sacred book of Confucius!

Messenger, when you were about to depart,
did the lady give you a special message
to deliver to me in person?

MESSENGER: As a matter of fact, sir,
she did.

CHANG: What did she say?

MESSENGER: She said to be sure to tell you
never on any account become involved
with another woman!

CHANG: Is that really what she said?

MESSENGER: Yes, really.

CHANG: Are you sure?

MESSENGER: I am sure.

CHANG: Well, then, you may go.

(*As the* MESSENGER *exits, the wind whistles and howls, and the rain comes down in torrents.*)

CHANG: (*Sings.*)

["The Wind Comes in Gusts"]
The wind comes in gusts,
and the rain beats down with a fury,
beats down.
The wind comes in gusts,
gusts, gusts,
and the rain beats down with a fury,
beats down with a fury,
with a fury beats down.

(*The wind and rain suddenly subside, and the moon emerges shining brightly. He resumes singing.*)

But our love will last
long after the mountains melt away
our love will last
long after the mountains melt away
our love will last . . .

(*Fade-out.*)

(LORD CHENG-HENG *in the courtyard of the eastern
pavilion.*)

LORD CHENG-HENG: (*Pompous.*)
Ying-ying's mourning period for her father is over,
so our marriage can take place.

But as I arrived in town, I heard upsetting news,
that Ying-ying's mother has betrothed her to another.
But she'd never do that.
I'm a very important person
from a very wealthy and very distinguished family.
Besides, Ying-ying cannot be engaged
to two men at the same time!

HONG-NIANG: (*Enters, bows.*) Lord Cheng-heng,
why you here?

LORD CHENG-HENG: Why, if it isn't Hong-niang,
the very person who can solve this dilemma.

HONG-NIANG: Dilemma? What dilemma?

LORD CHENG-HENG: The period of mourning
for the prime minister is over.
So I wanted to inform Lady Tsui
she may select the lucky day of marriage
for Ying-ying and me.
But I've heard
that Lady Tsui has also betrothed Ying-ying
to a student named Chang.
I must have been misinformed.

HONG-NIANG: You not misinform.
Ying-ying betroth to Mr. Chang,
scholar and poet.

LORD CHENG-HENG: But her father
betrothed her to me! Now that he is dead,
how can his widow go back on her husband's promise?

HONG-NIANG: Case not exactly as you say.
When Flying Tiger come with five thousand bandit,
Mr. Chang save life of everyone in monastery.
What if bandit carry off Ying-ying?

With who you now plead case?
No! Ying-ying rightfully belong to Mr. Chang.

LORD CHENG-HENG: *Belongs to* Mr. Chang!
Had she been betrothed to someone of her own class,
someone of a well-to-do and distinguished family,
I would not press to get what is rightfully mine.
But to give her to Chang—a poor starving beggar,
someone so beneath her—is intolerable!

HONG-NIANG: So, according you,
Mr. Chang not good as you.

LORD CHENG-HENG: You say five thousand bandits
came to the monastery.
How could Chang make so many men retreat?
The whole story is nothing but make-believe and
nonsense!

HONG-NIANG: No! Not make-believe!
Not nonsense! Flying Tiger and gang attack monastery!

LORD CHENG-HENG: What could one student do
against five thousand bandits?

HONG-NIANG: I tell you what he do!
At critical moment,
Lady Tsui pledge to give Ying-ying for wife
to man who make plan to drive bandit off.
Mr. Chang save day with plan.
He write letter to White Horse General,
who arrive quickly and put out fire!
Plan of Mr. Chang drive off bandit.
Mr. Chang win Ying-ying fair!

LORD CHENG-HENG: Who has ever heard
of Mr. Chang?
My family for generations has had no one but V.I.P.s!
Not unknowns! Not nobodies!

HONG-NIANG: Mr. Chang not nobody!
He devoted to understanding,
and respect very foundation of life,
and he gain fame through own effort.
You depend only on ancestor and rich family.
Whatever have, you given.
You not even know difference between right and wrong.
You say only son of official worthy become official.
Your scheme keep poor poor
while rich grow richer!
But history show many great men—
prime minister, military commander, poet—

come from poor home.
Tell me, sir,
would you know good man if saw one?

LORD CHENG-HENG: If I cannot have Ying-ying,
I will send twenty of my friends
to take her to my place by force,
where we will do with her as we please.
Then I will send her back to her mother,
who will be only too happy to have her become my wife!

HONG-NIANG: Ha! Mr. Chang never do that!
He philosopher of Confucian school.
He know decency,
and difference between right and wrong.
Compare to him, you firefly while he full moon!
You, very important man of very important family,
no better than bandit Flying Tiger!
All story I hear about you true!

LORD CHENG-HENG: What stories?
But there's no point in talking further.
I will marry her! Do you hear?
Marry her!

HONG-NIANG: She not marry you! Do you hear?
Not marry you!

She in love with young man smart and beautiful!
Nothing can make you smart,
and all makeup in world
not make you half as handsome as Mr. Chang!
He good and kind, strong and gentle, brave and
determine.
But, like you say, no point talk more.

LORD CHENG-HENG: Send for Lady Tsui!
I want to see her at once!

(HONG-NIANG *bows and exits*.)

LORD CHENG-HENG: I will tell Lady Tsui
that Chang passed the imperial examination
in first place,
and married
and became the son-in-law
of the Grand Chancellor of the Imperial University.
I like making people do what I want,
and I don't care how I go about it.
You will now see how I use this skill
to bring about my own happy marriage!

LADY TSUI: (*Enters.*) Good day, Lord Cheng-heng.
Hong-niang told me you were here.

LORD CHENG-HENG: (*Bows.*) Good day, Lady Tsui,
I will come quickly to the point.
I heard a rumor that in my absence
you betrothed Ying-ying to another.
Is it true?

LADY TSUI: Lord Cheng-heng,
surely you must have heard the rest of the story,
the terrible Flying Tiger business.
Ying-ying had no means of escaping the greatest of perils
without betrothal to Mr. Chang.

LORD CHENG-HENG: Mr. Chang? Which Mr. Chang?
Not the one who has just passed number one
on the imperial examination?
He is about twenty-three?—
comes from Lo-yang from a very poor family?

LADY TSUI: You know him?

LORD CHENG-HENG: Yes,
After the examination results were announced,
Mr. Chang married the Grand Chancellor's daughter,
whereupon he was appointed professor
in the Department of Chinese Literature
at the Imperial University in the capital.

LADY TSUI: Are you sure?
If, what you say is true, then you, Lord Cheng-heng,
as originally arranged,
will become my son-in-law!

(*Fade-out.*)

(*Courtyard of the monastery.*)

SUPERIOR: (*Enters in excitement.*) I have just seen
the list of successful candidates!
Our Scholar Chang has passed with honors
and is returning to us!
He has been appointed Governor of Ho-chung!
We must get ready and prepare a banquet
to celebrate this great and happy occasion!

LADY TSUI: (*Enters.*) Mr. Chang has deceived us!
He has married the daughter of the Grand Chancellor!
So Lord Cheng-heng is to become my son in-law.
Today is a lucky one for marriage,
and Lord Cheng-heng is expected at any moment.

CHANG: (*Off stage, singing "Sailed to the Sun." He enters, in splendid attire, continuing to sing.*)

[Reprise: "Sailed to the Sun"]
Sailed to the sun, sailed to the moon,
sailed to the sun and moon.
I have embarked upon a raft
and sailed to the sun and moon.

I return today in glory
after receiving by decree of the emperor
the exalted appointment of Governor of Ho-chung.

My literary ability, hitherto unrecognized,
has long been unequaled in the world.
But now I shall be famous.
Yesterday I was a poor student,
but now the emperor has promoted me
to membership in the Imperial Academy.
I may have looked like a fool to you,
but my dazzling brilliance
shines forth at last!

(*He bows to* LADY TSUI.)

Lady Tsui, I have passed the imperial examination
with high honors—

out of many I was number three—
and have been appointed Governor of Ho-chung.

LADY TSUI: Don't bow to me, sir! Don't bow!

CHANG: I don't understand!
I have attained everything you wanted of me.
So why are you displeased?

LADY TSUI: If it had not been
for the Flying Tiger incident,
which gave you an extraordinary opportunity,
it would have been out of the question
for you to consider
gaining entrance into our family!
And now you show utter disdain
for my daughter by marrying another!

CHANG: What scoundrel has told this monstrous lie?

LADY TSUI: Lord Cheng-heng told me
that you have become
the son-in-law of the Grand Chancellor.

HONG-NIANG: (*Enters.*) So Mr. Chang return
after pass examination and obtain high office!

CHANG: Hong-niang!
How is your young mistress?

HONG-NIANG: (*Angry.*) Why you care? (*Sings.*)

["Are You Happy Now?"]
Why you care?
Are you happy now, Mr. Chang?
Are you there?
What you thinking now, Mr. Chang?
Will you live in fancy neighborhood?
Will your life be better than good
in famous capital?

I tell you: You no care!
You are happy now, Mr. Chang!
I no care what you thinking now, Mr. Chang!
You go live in fancy neighborhood!
Think your life be better than good
in famous capital!
Now accept high position there!
Now breathe in perfumed city air!
Now no more care!

Are you happy now, Mr. Chang?
Are you there?
What you thinking now, Mr. Chang?

Will you live in fancy neighborhood?
Do you think you really so good
in famous capital?
Will you taste many banquet there?
Why come here? Why you care? Why you dare?
And tell me, Mr. Chang,
please tell me, Mr. Chang,
how does bride compare
with Ying-ying?

CHANG: Hong-niang, must you also talk nonsense?
If I have a bride in the capital or anywhere,
may I drop dead on the spot!
How could I ever forget moonlight in the western
chamber?
How could I abandon the one true love of my life?

YING-YING: (*Enters in her bridal gown, cooly to*
CHANG.)
Good wishes to you, sir!

CHANG: That's all?
Haven't you something else to say?

YING-YING: I prepared no end of things to say,
but now I cannot find a word.
Oh, yes. One.
Mr. Chang, I hear you've married another.
Is it true?

CHANG: Who told you that?

YING-YING: Lord Cheng-heng.

CHANG: Why does everyone listen to him
and not to me?   Ever since I left here,
I've not even glanced at another woman.
And yet, now I'm even accused of marrying
the Grand Chancellor's daughter!

HONG-NIANG: I knew not true!
Lord Cheng-heng tell big lie!

SUPERIOR: Lady Tsui, Mr. Chang
saved us all from a terrible massacre!
We were all witnesses to your promise,
so how can you possibly go back on your word?
Mr. Chang is an honorable man.
So what if he's not perfect?
You can't hold that against him.
Even the noblest hero has a bit of a devil in him!

TU: (*Enters.*) Lady Tsui, I've heard the good news!
My brother Chang Jun-rui
has been appointed Governor of Ho-chung
and is going to marry your daughter.
So I've come to offer congratulations!

LADY TSUI: But Lord Cheng-heng insists
Mr. Chang has become the son-in-law
of the Grand Chancellor, whereas Lord Cheng-heng,
whose father was Minister of Internal Affairs,
has remained faithful to his promise.

TU: But Lady Tsui, has no one told you
that Chang Jun-rui's father
was Minister of Internal Affairs
before Lord Cheng-heng's father obtained that position,
which he received when Chang's father died?
Besides, have you not heard of the scandal
concerning Lord Cheng-heng—
that he accepted bribes
and also stole money from the national treasury?

LORD CHENG-HENG: (*Enters dressed as a
bridegroom.*)
Here I am dressed to perfection,
ready to become Ying-ying's husband!

(*He bows before everyone individually. He stops before* CHANG, *scrutinizes him before bowing to him.*)

Why, if it isn't the genius of Lo-yang!
What a great honor for me, sir!
I heard you were first
on the imperial examination,
so I extend to you my most sincere congratulations!

(HUI *enters and hands* SUPERIOR *a note.*)

SUPERIOR: Attention, everyone!
I have just received an important announcement!
The daughter of the Grand Chancellor
has married the student taking first place
on the imperial examination!

(*The crowd murmurs.*)

LORD CHENG-HENG: See! What did I tell you?
Ying-ying is mine!

LADY TSUI: But wait! Mr. Chang did not place first!
Mr. Chang placed only third! Isn't that so, Mr. Chang?

CHANG: Yes, that is so.

LADY TSUI: So you're not married to the daughter
of the Grand Chancellor?

CHANG: That's what I've been trying to tell you!

LADY TSUI: Well, third place is not so bad . . .

SUPERIOR: I have another announcement.
Lord Cheng-heng has been accused of crimes
of a serious nature—taking bribes
and also stealing from the national treasury.
He is summoned by the emperor himself
to appear before him and answer these charges.

HONG-NIANG: See! What I tell you!
Ying-ying not become bride of bad man!

LADY TSUI: Lord Cheng-heng, please,
before everyone assembled here:
are the charges true?

HONG-NIANG: Why ask?
You already know he big liar!

LADY TSUI: Lord Cheng-heng,
you are about to marry my daughter!
I must have an answer!

Are the charges true?
The late prime minister approved your engagement
to our daughter because he was under the impression
you were an honorable man.
But now there is some doubt.
Lord Cheng-heng, cast away doubt and defend yourself!
Otherwise, I cannot approve this marriage!

LORD CHENG-HENG: (*Contemptuously.*) Lady Tsui,
by questioning me as you do
you reveal yourself as insolent and lowly
as your servant, Hong-niang!
And so, I no longer wish to marry your daughter.
I no longer wish to have anything more
to do with your family!
Before everyone assembled here,
I renounce my engagement to Ying-ying!
She may marry whoever is foolish enough
to marry her!
Now, if you will excuse me, I must go! (*Bows and exits.*)

ALL: We excuse you, Lord Cheng-heng!
Have a safe journey to the capital!
Have a pleasant meeting with the emperor!

TU: A cup of wine for Governor Chang
to make the first toast!

(HUI *hands* CHANG *a cup, which* CHANG *lifts.*)

CHANG: The first toast goes to Hong-niang,
the world's best matchmaker!

ALL: To Hong-niang! World's best matchmaker!

(CHANG *drinks and hands the cup back to* HUI.)

HONG-NIANG: Thank you!
But Mr. Chang, is there nothing more?

CHANG: Yes, there is more!

(HUI *hands* CHANG *a crown of flowers.   CHANG places it on* HONG-NIANG*'s head.   Then he gives her a full-length embroidered gown, which she holds up to the admiring throng, then exits with it.*   YING-YING *stands at* CHANG*'s side.*)

SUPERIOR: Today is the luckiest day
to have a marriage!
Four-horsed chariots crowd the gate!
The emperor's messenger and retinue are coming!
Mr. Chang has plucked the flower of success
from the moon!

YING-YING: (*Sings.*)

["Plucking the Flower of Success from the Moon"]
Four-horsed chariots crowd the gate
and eight young dragons adorn the door.
I marry my heart's true love and fulfill my life's desire.
I have plucked the flower of success
from the moon.

YING-YING and CHANG: (*Sing.*)

Four-horsed chariots crowd the gate
and eight young dragons adorn the door.
I marry my heart's true love and fulfill my life's desire.
We have plucked the flower of success
from the moon.

["Imperial Messenger's Fanfare"]

(HONG-NIANG *enters wearing floral crown and long gown. Everyone applauds.* IMPERIAL MESSENGER *fanfare is repeated and this time* IMPERIAL MESSENGER *enters.* ALL *bow.*)

IMPERIAL MESSENGER: I am the imperial messenger with a proclamation from the Emperor:

"Peace reigns throughout the land!
And even the mountains echo,
'Long live the Emperor!'"

ALL: Long live the Emperor!

IMPERIAL MESSENGER: "The people under heaven
are prosperous,
all the crops yield bountiful harvests,
and in every household is peace.
Everywhere happiness abides in the land.
And soon we shall see the coming
of the wondrous magic phoenix
and the glorious unicorn!

"By the grace of the wise Emperor
of the T'ang Dynasty,
a decree has been issued sanctioning
the marriage today of the lovers
Tsui Ying-ying and Chang Jun-rui.
May they live together
from now through old age
and then for all eternity!
And the Emperor hopes that all lovers
through the whole wide world
will marry so happily."

ALL: (*Sing.*)

> [Finale: "Through All Eternity"]
> May they live together through all eternity,
> and may all lovers through the world
> marry so happily!
>
> And soon we shall see
> the coming of the wondrous magic phoenix
> and the glorious unicorn,
> which will mark the coming
> of a long and prosperous age!
>
> May they live together through all eternity,
> and may all lovers through the world
> marry so happily!

(DANCERS *and* ACROBATS *enter and perform.*)

(*Blackout.*)

THE END

ABOUT THE AUTHOR

HOWARD RUBENSTEIN is a physician and a writer. He was born in 1931 in Chicago, where he graduated from Lake View High School. He received a B.A. from Carleton College, where he was elected to Phi Beta Kappa and Sigma Xi and won the Noyes Prize for excellence in ancient Greek. Rubenstein received an M.D. from Harvard Medical School. In 1967 he was appointed Physician and Chief of Allergy at the Harvard University Health Services. In 1989 he was appointed a Medical Consultant to the Department of Social Services, state of California. In 2000 he retired from the practice of medicine.

Howard Rubenstein's translation of Aeschylus' *Agamemnon* was produced by the Granite Hills Acting Workshop in 1997. P. E. Easterling, Regius Professor of Greek, University of Cambridge, England, gave the translation a glowing review, calling it "lively . . . vigorous . . . [with] great directness . . . accessible to modern audiences." A videotape of the production was requested by Oliver Taplin, Regius Professor, Oxford, and may be found in the Archive of Performances of Greek and Roman Drama, University of Oxford. Rubenstein's translation of Euripides' *The Trojan Women* was produced in 2001, and was the most decorated show (*San Diego Playbill*) of the 2000–2001 San Diego theater season. Rubenstein has also written scientific papers, "Maccabee" an epic in free verse, and other books.